Praise for

C000144048

PHILIP PULLMAN

IMAGINARY FRIENDS

In answer to Richard Dawkins's assertion that fairy tales may have a pernicious effect on children, with reference to the author's own experience of reading and imagining.

David Fickling Books

'Imaginary Friends', from *Dæmon Voices: Essays on Storytelling*
is a
DAVID FICKLING BOOK

First published in Great Britain in 2017 by
David Fickling Books,
31 Beaumont Street,
Oxford, OX1 2NP

Imaginary Friends text © Philip Pullman, 2017
Introduction text © Simon Mason, 2017

978-1-910989-93-7

1 3 5 7 9 10 8 6 4 2

The right of Philip Pullman and Simon Mason to be identified as the authors of this work
has been asserted in accordance with the Copyright, Designs and Patents Act 1988.

Papers used by David Fickling Books are from well-managed forests and other respon-
sible sources.

DAVID FICKLING BOOKS Reg. No. 8340307

A CIP catalogue record for this book is available from the British Library.

Printed and bound in UK

Introduction

'Imaginary Friends' is one of the thirty-three pieces collected in Dæmon Voices: Essays on Storytelling.

It is an excellent example of Philip's essay-writing. He begins with a book he has been reading – in this case Richard Dawkins' The Magic of Reality. *Many of the essays in the collection were prompted by Philip's reading – of Grimm's folk tales, Milton's* Paradise Lost, *Blake's poetry or the wonderful little essay by Heinrich von Kleist, 'On the Marionette Theatre' – a major inspiration for* His Dark Materials.

'Imaginary Friends' is typical too in its relaxed tone and easy accessibility. Though his

essays often deal with complex ideas, the essays themselves are never in the least obscure.

Typical too is the curiosity and open-mindedness with which he asks the apparently simple question: how do children read fairy tales? In all his essays, with great energy and interest, he engages ideas and issues, and asks interesting questions. Is the world conscious? What is our place and purpose here? What is evil? Can innocence be regained?

But the subject he returns to most, the one which fascinates him the most, is the one he knows most about: storytelling itself. Together, in fact, the essays form a single, sustained engagement with story and storytelling by one of the great storytellers.

Simon Mason,
Editor of *Dæmon Voices*
2017

IMAGINARY FRIENDS

Richard Dawkins's book, *The Magic of Reality*, is a tour de force in which he tells a number of myths (about, for instance, the creation of the earth, or rainbows, or where animals came from) and then gives a scientific account of the phenomenon in question, showing how thrilling knowledge and scientific inquiry can be and what a profound sense of wonder they can give us. It's a book that I shall certainly give to my grandchildren in a year or two. I have never seen a better introduction to science for young readers.

But it reminded me of Dawkins's misgivings, expressed in a TV news interview two or three years ago, about such things as fairy tales in which frogs turn into princes. He said he would like to know of any evidence about the results of telling children stories like that: did it have a pernicious effect? In particular, he worried that it might lead to an anti-scientific cast of mind, in which people were prepared to believe that things could change into other things. And because I have been working on the tales of the Brothers Grimm recently, the matter of fairy tales and the way we read them has been much on my mind.

So, what evidence might there be to settle this question?

We believe different things in different ways

and for different reasons. There's the rock-hard certainty of personal experience ('I put my finger in the fire and it hurt'), which is probably the earliest kind we learn. Then there's the logically convincing, which we probably come to through the maths we learn at school, in the context of Pythagoras's theorem or something similar, and which, if we first encounter it at the right moment, bursts on our minds like sunrise, with the whole universe playing a great chord of C major.

However, there are other ways of believing that things are true, such as the testimony of trusted friends ('I know him and he's not a liar'), the plausibility of likelihood based on experience ('It's exactly the sort of thing you'd expect to happen'), the blind conviction of the religious zealot ('It must be true, because God says so and His holy book doesn't lie'), the placid assent of those who like a quiet life ('If you say so, dear'), and so on. Some of these carry within them the possibility of quiet scepticism ('I know him and he's not a liar – but he might be mistaken').

There's not just one way of believing in things but a whole spectrum. We don't demand or require scientific proof of everything we believe, not only because it would be impossible to provide but because, in a lot of cases, it isn't necessary or appropriate.

How could we examine children's experience of fairy tales? Are there any models for examining children's experience of story in a reasonably objective way? As it happens, there are. A very interesting study was carried out some years ago by a team led by Gordon Wells and his colleagues at Bristol University and was described in a book called *The Meaning Makers: Children Learning Language and Using Language to Learn* (Hodder, 1986).

Wells and his team wanted to find out how children's language was influenced by what they heard around them. They selected a large number of families with children who were two or three years old, whom they followed right up to the end of their primary education, giving the children unobtrusive, lightweight radio microphones, to be worn under their clothes, which could pick up not only what the children said but also what was being said by parents or others nearby. The microphones were switched on at random intervals for ninety seconds at a time, the results were recorded and transcribed and then an enormous amount of analysis was done on the results.

In brief, they discovered that the more included children were in the conversation and chatter going on around them, the quicker and more fully they picked up every kind of language skill. One interesting discovery was that the most enriching experience of all was the open-ended exploratory talk that arises from the reading of stories. In *Language and Learning: an International Perspective* (1985), Wells and his colleague John Nicholls write: 'Several investigators have noted how much more complex, semantically and syntactically, is the language that occurs in this context . . . Furthermore, the frequency with which children are read to has been found to be a powerful predictor of later success at school.'

So, it's not impossible to set up experiments to test how children acquire various forms of understanding and to learn interesting things from them. But to go back to Dawkins and his question, how on earth would we set up an experiment to test the effect of fairy tales?

It would have to go on much longer than the Bristol study: it would have to last as long as childhood itself. And it would have to differ from that study in an important way, because it would need a control group. Whereas the scholars at Bristol were concerned with finding out what happens in the natural course of a child's life, this study would depend on having some children who were allowed fairy tales, fantasy and so on, and another group that wasn't.

To make it absolutely beyond question, it would have to be policed pretty rigorously. No *Harry Potter* under the bedclothes. No nursery rhymes either, which are full of impossible things, such as cows jumping over the moon. And we would follow the children all the way through their schooling, right up to leaving age, to see whether the ones who were kept away from magic and spells were thereby advantaged in their understanding of science.

Of course, we wouldn't do it. It would amount to child abuse. To make sure that our subjects never encountered fairy tales of any kind, we would have to keep them in a sort of prison camp. Dawkins knows this; he wouldn't ask for the unreasonable, or the impossible, or the cruel. When he says that he would like to see some evidence, I assume that he is prepared to be a little generous in his view of what evidence there could be.

And the only way we can know what is going on in the mind of someone who reads a story is to believe them when they tell us about it and compare it with our own experience of reading and see what we have in common. When it comes to the matter that Dawkins is concerned about, namely the question of children's belief in fairy tales and magic and spells, all we have to go by is belief and trust. It's that sort of evidence, and that's the only sort we've got – but then, we get by pretty well with that in most of our dealings with other people.

So, do children believe what they read in stories, or don't they? And if they do, in what way do they believe it? Well, this is what I think about it. I think that childhood reading is more like play than like anything else. Like pretending. When I was a boy of eight or nine, in Australia, we pretended to be figures from comics or films and we acted out stories based on the adventures we'd seen. Davy Crockett was very big at that time – every little boy in the western world had a Davy Crockett hat. I knew I wasn't really Davy Crockett but, at the same time, I liked imitating things that I'd seen Davy Crockett do on the cinema screen – say, at the Siege of the Alamo.

We fought with passion, and when we died

we did so with heroic extravagance. My body was doing all that an eight-year-old body could do to run out from behind a wall, fire a musket, clutch my chest, stagger, crumple to the ground, slowly drag a revolver from a holster with a trembling hand and kill six Mexicans as I breathed my last.

Those were the things my body was doing. What was my mind doing? I think it was feeling a little scrap – a tiny, fluttering, tattered, cheaply printed, torn-off scrap – of heroism. I felt what it was like to be brave and to die facing overwhelming odds. That intensity of feeling is what both fuels and rewards childhood play and reading alike. When we children play at being characters we admire, doing things we value, we discover in doing so areas and depths of feeling it would be hard to reach otherwise. Exhilaration, heroism, despair, resolution, triumph, noble renunciation, sacrifice: in acting these out, we experience them in miniature or, as it were, in safety.

Yet at no time during the endless hours of play I spent as a child did I believe that I was anyone other than myself. Sometimes I was me and sometimes I was me pretending to be Davy Crockett. But now that I think about it carefully, I realise that it was a little more complicated than that. When I was playing with my brother and my friends, I was almost entirely Crockett, or Batman, or Dick Tracy, or whoever it was (and I remember games when there were about six different Batmans racing through the neighbourhood gardens). It was when I played alone that I found it possible to be myself, but a different myself, a myself who was Davy Crockett's close and valued friend, who sat with him beside a campfire in the wilderness or hunted bears in the trackless forests of suburban Adelaide. Sometimes I rescued him from danger and sometimes he rescued me, but we were both pretty laconic about it. In some ways, I was more myself at those times than at any other – a stronger and more certain myself, wittier, more clearly defined, a myself of accomplishment and renown, someone Davy Crockett could rely on in a tight spot.

What's more, he seemed to value me more than my friends and family did. He saw the qualities in me that their duller eyes failed to perceive. Davy Crockett wasn't alone in this

superior perception; I remember that King
Arthur had a high opinion of me, and so did
Superman.

Now I think that those experiences were
an important part of my moral education as
well as the development of my imagination. By
acting out stories of heroism and sacrifice and
(to use a fine phrase that has become a cliché)
grace under pressure, I was building patterns of
behaviour and expectation into my moral
understanding. I might fall short if ever I were
really called on, but at least I'd know what was
the right thing to do.

And that sort of play, the solitary play,
perhaps, even more than the communal play,
seems to me very similar to what we do when
we read – at least when we read for no other

purpose than our enjoyment, and especially when we read as children. I'm conscious that the way I read as an adult is a little different, because there's a part of my reading mind now that looks with critical attention at the way the story is told as well as at the events it relates.

What I thought mostly when I was a child was, 'I want to be in this story with them.' It was like the sort of game where I was by myself with Davy Crockett in the wilderness, because in a story I was able to be both myself here and myself there. I didn't want to stop being myself; I didn't want to be them; I wanted to put myself into the story and enjoy things happening to me. And in the private, secret, inviolable space that opened out miraculously between the printed page and my young mind, that sort of thing happened all the time. It's the state of mind in which you can hear the voice of your dæmon. In fact, there are probably dæmon voices whispering to us all the time, and we've forgotten how to hear them.

I remember it happening especially powerfully with the Moomins. Little creatures who looked like miniature hippopotamuses and lived on an island in the Baltic Sea? Absurd. What I felt for the Moomin family and all their friends, however, was nothing less than love. In fact, I loved them so much that I would never have said to my friends, 'Let's pretend we're Moomins.' That would have been inconceivable. I would have had to make public something I felt private and secret about, something I could hardly voice even to myself, something which – were it ever discovered – I would have felt embarrassed by; and the shame of discovery, I'm sure, would have been followed quickly by the even greater and longer-lasting shame of betrayal. To save face, I'd have felt obliged to mock and scoff at those dear friends of mine, and at any kid who was so stupid and babyish as to like stories about them.

But when I was alone, with a Moomin book open in front of me and that great, secret space opening up between my mind and the pages, I could revel in their company and sail off in their floating theatre or travel to the mountains to see the great comet or rescue the Snork Maiden from the Groke and no one could possibly have told, from looking at me, what my mind was doing.

Here comes the test: did I believe that the Moomins were real? No, of course I didn't. I knew that they were made up. I was pretending they were real in order to enjoy being with them in imagination. I wasn't in the slightest danger of confusing them with real life. The delight of being with the Moomins was a complex kind of delight, made up partly of the sweetness of their characters, partly of the delicate, simple precision of the drawings, partly of the endless inventiveness of Tove Jansson, their creator, partly from the fascination I felt with the northern landscape in which they lived: a whole bundle of things, none of which depended on their being true or real.

Nor did I believe for a second that elephants' trunks were long because one of their ancestors

had played a desperate tug of war with a crocodile, as Rudyard Kipling told me in the *Just So
Stories*. If someone had asked me, in a serious
kind of way, why I thought elephants had long
trunks, I'd have scratched my head and said, 'I
dunno.' I knew, even when I was very young,
that 'because the crocodile got hold of the elephant's child's nose and pulled and pulled' was
the wrong sort of answer.

I would have been just as fascinated, in a
different kind of way, to hear the real answer;
but that wouldn't have diminished my pleasure
in the story, which included the delight that I
felt in murmuring the sounds of the words: the
'satiable curtiosity' of the elephant's child, the
'great, grey-green, greasy Limpopo River, all
set about with fever trees'. I knew these story

things, these play things, weren't real, but that didn't matter, because I didn't want them to be real, I wanted them to be funny. Or delightful. Or exciting. Or moving. And they could be all those things and real as well, as some things were, or all those things and imaginary and I could tell the difference, and it didn't matter.

I agree that it would be a different question entirely if parents actually brought their children up to believe that frogs could change into princes. And some parents do bring their children up to believe that things can change into other things – bread into flesh and wine into blood, to be specific, and that they'll go to hell if they don't believe it. Some parents also bring their children up to believe that the world was created 6,000 years ago and that scientists are wrong when they tell us about evolution and shouldn't be allowed to teach it in schools. I fully agree with Dawkins when he says that this is pernicious and damaging.

Yet there's a world of difference between that sort of thing and offering a child a fairy tale. No one says, 'You must believe that the frog changed into a prince, because it's true and only wicked people don't believe it.' Children really do learn quite early on that there are different ways of believing in different kinds of story.

And when it comes to evidence, I think there's nothing for it: we just have to trust what people tell us and check it against our own experience. If what they say is that stories of every kind, from the most realistic to the most fanciful, have nourished their imagination and helped shape their moral understanding, then we have to accept the truth of that. My guess is that the kind of stories children are offered has far less effect on their development than whether they are given stories at all; and that children whose parents take the trouble to sit and read with them – and talk about the stories, not in a lecturing sort of way but genuinely conversing, in the way that Gordon Wells describes – will grow up to be much more fluent and confident not only with language, but with pretty well any kind of intellectual activity, including science. And children who are deprived of this contact, this interaction, the world of stories, are not likely to flourish at all.

What sort of evidence that is, I don't know, but I believe it.

This article first appeared in the New Statesman, *13 December 2011.*

Dæmon Voices

In over thirty essays, written over twenty years, one of the world's great storytellers meditates on storytelling. Warm, funny, generous, entertaining and, above all, deeply considered, they offer thoughts on a wide variety of topics, including the origin and composition of Philip's own stories, the craft of writing and the storytellers who have meant the most to Philip.

The art of storytelling is everywhere present in the essays themselves, in the instantly engaging tone, the vivid imagery and striking phrases, the resonant anecdotes, the humour and learnedness. Together, they are greater than the sum of their parts: a single, sustained engagement with story and storytelling.

Dæmon Voices: Essays on Storytelling by Philip Pullman is published by David Fickling Books on 2 November 2017.

The Book of Dust

Philip Pullman returns to the world of *His Dark Materials* for a new major trilogy. *The Book of Dust* is a work in three parts, like *His Dark Materials*. Published jointly by David Fickling Books and Penguin Random House Children's in the UK, and by Random House Children's in the US.

Philip Pullman said: "The first thing to say is that Lyra is at the centre of the story. Events involving her open the first chapter, and will close the last.

"So, second: is it a prequel? Is it a sequel? It's neither. In fact, *The Book of Dust* is an 'equel'. It doesn't stand before or after *His Dark Materials*, but beside it.

"Third: why return to Lyra's world? Dust. The idea of Dust suffused *His Dark Materials*".

The first volume of Philip Pullman's *The Book of Dust* is published on Thursday 19th October 2017.

About the Author

PHILIP PULLMAN is one of the most acclaimed writers working today. He is best known for the *His Dark Materials* trilogy (*Northern Lights, The Subtle Knife, The Amber Spyglass*), which has been named one of the top 100 novels of all time by *Newsweek*. He has also won many distinguished prizes, including the Carnegie Medal for *Northern Lights* (and the reader-voted "Carnegie of Carnegies" for the best children's book of the past seventy years); the Whitbread (now Costa) Award for *The Amber Spyglass*; and the Astrid Lindgren Memorial Award, in honour of his body of work.

Philip Pullman lives in Oxford, England. To learn more, please visit www.philip-pullman.com or follow him on Twitter at @PhilipPullman.